IMAGES
of America

RESORTS OF
LAKE COUNTY

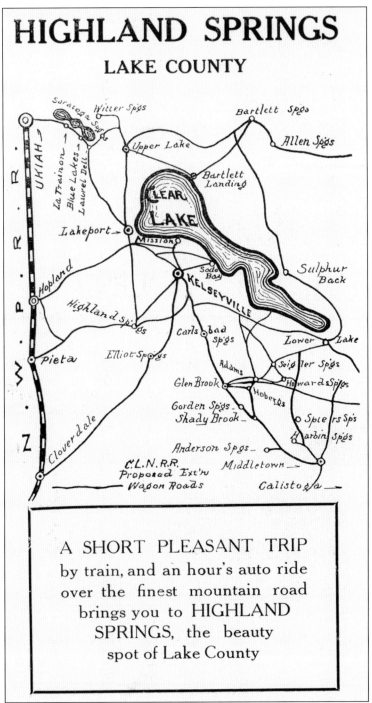

The above map of Lake County is from a Highland Springs brochure around 1920 and shows many of the resorts that were in business at that time.

ON THE COVER: A group of California Camera Club members are at Blue Lakes Resort on their way to Seigler Springs Resort in 1918. (Courtesy Darlene Hecomovich.)

IMAGES
of America

RESORTS OF
LAKE COUNTY

Donna Hoberg

ARCADIA
PUBLISHING

Published by Arcadia Publishing
Charleston SC, Chicago IL, Portsmouth NH, San Francisco CA

Printed in the United States of America

Library of Congress Catalog Card Number: 2007925811

For all general information contact Arcadia Publishing at:
Telephone 843-853-2070
Fax 843-853-0044
E-mail sales@arcadiapublishing.com
For customer service and orders:
Toll-Free 1-888-313-2665

Visit us on the Internet at www.arcadiapublishing.com

Pictured are charter buses arriving at Hoberg's Resort c. 1950.

CONTENTS

ACKNOWLEDGMENTS

Many thanks to the Lake County Historical Society and to Linda Lake, curator of the Lake County Museum, for their generosity in allowing me to use their photograph archives, and to Pat Brown, project director of the museum's Historical Digitization Project, who helped me access those photographs that make up about half of this book. All other photographs came from friends and old-time acquaintances who were pleased to loan their postcard collections or pictures and share their memories. For this, I am grateful to my donors, Darlene Hecomovich, Marilyn Angelley, Don and Dorothy Emerson, Bruce and Pam Anderson, David Neft, Steve and Michaela Strickler, Jennifer Prather, Douglas Prather, Julie Kimelman, Larry Rogers, Gaylord Starin, Reggie Tantarelli, Jeff Gospe, Jennie Rossotti, Bob and Roberta Grahn, Richard Matzinger, Don Hoberg, Dave Hoberg, and Devin Hoberg. My special thanks go to Jeff Lorenzen, computer wizard, for his patient tutoring.

INTRODUCTION

The first resorts in Lake County began with the discovery of the mineral springs that were found in various regions throughout the county and on stage routes that linked Lake County with adjacent areas. The springs' development began as early as the late 1860s by making the waters available to tourists for drinking and bathing and establishing campgrounds. The first lodging constructed were small, crude cabins, but that changed quite quickly as the springs' popularity grew. Many of the immigrants who flooded into California in the mid-1880s were form the eastern states and settled in the Bay Area, believed in the cures that mineral waters offered, and were anxious to visit health spa facilities. With business booming, the early entrepreneurs were able to build hotels and more-comfortable accommodations and, in time, offered more recreational facilities. About the same time, a few resorts without hot springs were built at strategic spots along the stage roads coming into the county where the stage would stop to rest their horses and give the passengers a break. These resorts offered relaxation, recreation, and good food as well as accommodations.

In the area in the hills northeast of Clear Lake, four springs resorts were built: Bartlet, Allen, Hough and Newman—Bartlett Springs being the largest by far. These all contained multiple springs of varying temperatures and mineral content. To the east of this group sat Witter and Saratoga who also had multiple springs. On the road running to Ukiah from Upper lake were three early resorts on Blue Lakes that had no hot springs. On the west side of Clear Lake, about mid-way between the north and south shores, is Soda Bay, where hot springs came bubbling from the lake bottom and around the edge of the bay. Soda Bay Resort was established in 1872.

In the southern volcanic area of the county, some of the early hot springs resorts were Seigler, Howard, Adams, and Bonanza, and nearer to Middletown were Harbin and Anderson. Highland Springs was located west of Kelseyville on a stage road that came into the county from Hopland and continued on to Lakeport. In Cobb Valley, Glenbrook resort sat on the stage road halfway between Middletown and Lakeport. Glenbrook had no hot springs.

Recreation was not the most important asset of the spring's resorts in the beginning. Guests came to drink the water and bathe in it. They walked and relaxed, and since health was the foremost issue, most resorts began to provide healthy food and advertise quality "table." Health claims ran amok. Testimonials were common in their advertising, some with doctor's names attached. It was said that by drinking the mineral waters you could cure most ailments known at that time. The water was so popular that some of these businesses began hauling barrels of it to the Bay Area market by mule train. They also bottled the water and thousands of cases of Lake County bottled water were sold all over California and other parts of the United States. Between 1903 and 1914 mineral water was the major mineral extracted in Lake County.

The popularity of Lake County health resorts lasted about 50 years, before more modern times and less trust in the health claims of mineral waters began to affect the numbers of tourists who came just for their health. Tourists continued to come into Lake County, but they were looking for recreational facilities primarily, and as Lake County's population grew, more resorts without mineral springs were built. The state and county began improving the roads, and the new roads that were built left some of the older resorts too isolated, making it difficult for guests to reach their facilities and affecting the resorts' ability to stay in business. Sometimes they were defeated by disastrous fires or poor management. There were resorts, however, that combined their springs features with multiple recreational facilities and continued to operate into the 1960s.

By the 1920s and 1930s, small resorts offering housekeeping facilities and known as tourist camps had sprung up all around Clear Lake and in other areas. These provided economical lodging and some recreational facilities, but often the recreational opportunities were nearby. Campgrounds with minimal facilities were very popular and often offered only a creek or a pool if they were not near Clear Lake. Campgrounds were sometimes combined with cabins, and there would be a small store and restaurant.

American-plan resorts in the Cobb area, such as Hobergs, Forest Lake, Seiglers, and Adams, were a popular destination for people looking for rates that included their meals and provided not only recreational facilities but also entertainment. Adams and Seiglers were among the earliest springs developments that managed to stay in business by increasing their recreational and entertainment capabilities. These resorts all accommodated conventions during the spring and fall months and hosted many Lions clubs, Rotary clubs, telephone pioneers, the Redwood Empire Association, credit unions, garden clubs, and Organ clubs, to name but a few.

During World War II, the Bay Area was crowded by workers who came from all over the United States to produce warships and process munitions. The easy three-hour drive to Lake County made it an attractive destination. Employees from all the factories and ship yards could drive easily to Lake County for weekends away, and they were ready to party and play, or just to relax. Whatever their choice, Lake County resorts had lots to offer.

By the end of the 1950s, the popularity of the large resorts was fading. Tourists were traveling farther, enabled by cheap airfare, good roads, and better cars. The larger resorts that had accommodated conventions for many years as well as continuing to welcome summer guests began to feel the competition from afar. Most cities in the state were building convention facilities, and costs were rising. By the late 1960s, all of the larger resorts had been subdivided or sold for other business purposes. The heydays of the health resorts and the large recreational resorts were over. The smaller resorts did not suffer the same fate. There are 50 resorts listed in the business directory at this writing, and there is no doubt that beautiful Lake County will continue to attract tourists.

This early photograph shows a family outside the hot sulfur-spring bathhouse at Seigler Springs resort.

One

NORTH EAST HILLS

STAGES LEAVING BARTLETT SPRINGS.

In an area northeast of Clear Lake in the hills, four resorts were developed in the 1870s. Bartlett Springs was located by Green Bartlett, and he and L. Tharp filed claim in 1870 for certain mineral springs designated as Bartlett Springs. In 1872, they patented 160 acres around the springs and began building crude cabins. By 1875, there were 75 cabins and tents and a two-story hotel. In the beginning, the resort primarily catered to guests who came in response to the belief in the curative powers of the waters for diseases of the kidneys, liver, stomach, and bladder, and for rheumatism, dyspepsia, malaria, and more. The resort became one of the greatest natural sanitariums of the world. The stages pictured above carried people to and from Williams to the east or to and from Bartlett's Clear Lake landing, where they came across the lake from the west shore.

These ladies are gathered at the main Bartlett spring.

As the years went on, Bartlett Springs grew into a small town with hotels, markets, butcher shop, and rooms to accommodate 5,000 people. There was a dance hall, bowling alley, croquet court, tennis courts, and more. This photograph shows the Calvin Hotel, one of the hotels at the resort.

Calvin Hotel, Bartlett Springs Calif.

Bartlett was reporting their bottling figures as early as 1888 to the U.S. Geological Survey. The waters were hauled by wagons to San Francisco and Sacramento for shipment to markets around the world. Eventually the water was shipped to Honolulu, Alaska, and Central America, and it was the only soda water served on the Cunard and White Star ocean liners at one time. The picture above shows the crew at the bottling plant. In the photograph below, the wagons are loaded and ready to haul cases of Barlett water to market.

1618

Bottled water bottle wrapped for shipment

The photograph above shows the pavilion where guests could sit and drink the waters and enjoy visiting with friends. The picture to the right shows a bottle wearing its protective tulle wrapper for shipping.

The above picture shows one of the many stores that sold supplies to the guests who came to the village of Bartlett Springs. The motor stages shown below replaced the horse-drawn conveyances bringing guests to and from the resort. The roads may have been improved, but it was still a rough, dusty, dirt track that they had to travel.

The above advertisement is from a 1930s vacation guide published by Peck-Judah Travel Agency.

Pictured is one of the beautiful old hotels at Bartlett.

This photograph gives only a hint of what Hough Springs looked like from 1882 to 1930 when it prospered as a resort. The springs were located by Sulvaness Hough on the north side of Cache Creek on the Bear Valley and Bartlett Springs Toll Road and were sold to John Hugh Stratford in 1880. He built a large hotel, cottages, and campgrounds and maintained a store and post office. There were four springs, all cold at around 60 degrees, with various mineral content. The guests came mostly to improve their health. By the 1930s, the resort was abandoned.

Pool - Newman Springs

Newman Springs was a small resort developed by Swan W. Young, a Swedish immigrant who purchased the property from Mr. Newman in 1898. It was located one and a half miles north of Bartlett Springs. There were nine springs issuing along the channel of Soap Creek. The main spring yielded about 15 gallons a minute of mildly carbonated, 86-degree water that contained iron. A spring about 75 yards above this main spring formed a borax pool containing warm, turbid water considered to be excellent for bathing. Above, a group of bathers enjoys the waters of the walled-in swimming pool.

This photograph shows a portion of the Newman Springs resort. A disastrous fire burned the resort to the ground and it was never rebuilt. Young remained the owner of the property until his death in 1950.

The two-story hotel above was built over the stream at the Allen Springs resort, located three miles east of Bartlett Springs. There were five cool, carbonated springs issuing from or near Cache Creek above the hotel, and early on, they began bottling the water. The springs were discovered in 1871 by George and Vale Allen, who built a two-story hotel, 21 cottages, dance hall, billiard room, barbershop, general store, and stable over the next few years. There was a post office and Wells Fargo office connecting to the Bay Area by Western Union Telegraph. In 1881, the resort was sold to James D. Bailey. Most of the guests came to improve their health or for relaxation. By 1940, the resort facilities were abandoned.

Pictured to the right is a label used on bottles of Allen water sold for medicinal purposes as well as table water.

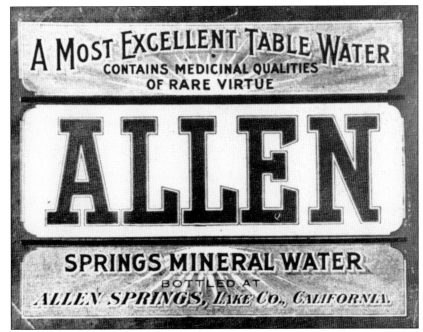

These guests
are enjoying the
Allen Springs
Club veranda.

In 1964, Allen Springs was in ruins.

Two

BLUE LAKES AND NEARBY

Three small, deep lakes known as Blue Lakes and located on the road from Ukiah six miles from Upper Lake gave rise to three very early resorts known as Le Trinon, Blue Lakes, and Laurel Dell. There were no hot springs at these three, but Witter Springs was located just to the northeast and Saratoga Springs lay just south of Witter. These two latter spring resorts were part of the mineral spring complex of Lake County. The photograph above shows an overview of one of the lakes, each about one and a half miles long, surrounded by steep mountains. The earliest Blue Lake resort lodge was built about 1870 by Ebenezer A. Graham, who also built the toll road. In 1880, Theodore Deming bought the hotel and stage stop, and by 1896, the resort included a pavilion over the water. The hotel was destroyed by fire in 1890 and rebuilt by Deming by 1899. It burned again and was rebuilt around 1913 when owned by the widow of Otto Weisman. In 1925, Harry and Maud Kemp purchased the resort, and later it became known as Pine Acres Resort Hotel.

Henry Wambold lived on the property he called Laurel Dell as early as 1873, and in 1878, the land was surveyed and Wambold started the resort with cottages between the toll road and the most southern Blue Lake. In 1890, he built a small hotel, and in 1900, he built a large hotel. The photograph above shows the resort from across the lake. Pictured below is the dining room built over the lake.

Laurel Dell Resort was surrounded by pepperwood and huge bay laurel trees along the lake shore. In 1896, a small steamer was available to guests to explore the lakes, and they could enjoy fishing, bathing, bowling, and tennis. Owner Henry Wambold built a two-story cannery for string beans nearby about 1891. By 1901, he sold his resort to Edgar Durnan and ran his cannery. The above photograph shows the large hotel at Laurel Dell on the left, and pictured below are the employees who worked in the dining room about 1900.

This 1890s lithograph shows an early view of Le Trianon Resort on Blue Lakes.

Le Trianon Resort pictured above, was built about 1875 and named after the summer palace Le Petit Trianon of the famous French queen Marie Antoinette.

Saratoga Springs was located in 1871 by J. W. Pearson, who filed claim for 160 acres; by 1879, there was a hotel known as Pearson's Springs. There were 12 springs of various mineral content on the property developed for drinking or bathing. Pearson sold to J. J. Kebert, who sold to James Wright in 1889, who sold to John Martens in 1896. Cottages were added and the hotel was rebuilt after a disastrous fire, and by 1910, there were accommodations for 250 guests with fully developed recreational facilities. The above photograph shows a group of guests in front of the hotel.

This photograph is of the hotel at Saratoga Springs.

Saratoga Mineral Springs
On Ukiah-Tahoe Highway

Situated in a miniature valley, free from winds and mosquitos. The hotel and cottages front large level grounds, well shaded. Elevation 1500 feet, insuring cool nights. The springs are all cold and carbonated, pleasing to the taste, consist of Sulphur, Magnesia, Soda, Arsenic, Seltzer, Iron, Surprise, Digester and Appetizer. Cool mineral plunge, water highly carbonated, very invigorating. Bring your bathing suits. Hot mineral tub baths 50c. Croquet, tennis, shuffle board, billiards, dancing. Mountain trails, affording fine views of valleys and Clear Lake, 7 miles distant. Electric lights throughout. Store, post office, telephone.

Hotel rates, $20.00 to $30.00 per week, children according to service required. Housekeeping cottages, furnished except silverware and towels, $15 per week. Reached via N. W. P. R. R. Purchase round trip tickets to Ukiah, 90-day limit, $5.55; 16-day limit on sale Friday, Saturday and Sunday, $4.60. From Ukiah take Pickwick stages to the Springs, fare one way $1.75; round trip $2.65. Pickwick stages leave San Francisco for the Springs. Round trip $7.90.

E. R. KEIL, Owner
Bachelor, Lake County, California

Descriptive matter and reservations without charge at Peck-Judah Travel Bureaus. Please mention Peck-Judah when writing this Resort.

The above advertisement is from a 1930 vacation guide published by Peck-Judah Travel Agency.

Witter springs were discovered by Benjamin Burke in 1870 and sold to Dr. Dexter Witter and W. P. Radcliff the following year. The original hotel and 13 cottages were built, and a medicinal resort was gradually built up. The principal spring, known as Deadshot Spring, issued from crevices in a massive rock in a ravine at the creek edge and yielded about 5/8 gallon per minute. It was 53 degrees and strongly carbonated with a saline taste, and its name made reference to the action of the water on diseases for which it was recommended. It was said to cure fits, scrofula, cancer, salt rheum, tetter, scald head, white swelling, rheumatism, neuralgia, dyspepsia, and all affections of the heart, kidneys, and liver. The photograph above is looking west from Bachelor Valley, and pictured below is the Witter ranch house.

In 1906, the magnificent Witter Hotel, pictured, was built containing 100 rooms and an exceptionally long veranda. This hotel was surrounded by 1,400 acres of land on which livestock, dairy products, fruits, and vegetables were raised. Unfortunately the cost of the beautiful hotel overextended the owners' finances, and with the decrease of guests due to the 1906 earthquake, they were forced into bankruptcy by 1915. The $250,000 hotel was sold for $15,000 dollars and salvaged. Various companies continued to sell bottled Witter water into the 1950s.

Pictured above is a view of the long veranda Witter Hotel was noted for.

Three

LAKEPORT AREA

Resorts in the Lakeport area were situated mostly along the lakeshores, where tourists could enjoy many water-related activities. Rainbow Camp, north of Lakeport, pictured, was one of the motor courts that sprang up along Clear Lake to accommodate the tourist trade requiring housekeeping units. These small resorts offered sandy beaches, boat rentals, fishing piers, and shady places to relax. They attracted tourists with limited budgets and were an important part of the changing scene from grand-scale health resorts to self-catering facilities.

Rainbow Camp, pictured in the above overview, was conveniently near Clear Lake's shores. It had a nice sandy beach, and with the cabins nearby, it was a wonderful place for families to enjoy their summer vacations. Catfish and bass were plentiful for those wishing to try their luck from the pier, pictured below, or in a small boat farther out on the lake.

Beach Scene at Camp Rainbow - Lakeport, Calif.

8086

Bonnie Brae Camp, pictured above and below, was situated along the north shore of Clear Lake. Tourists came in the summer to camp and enjoy the lake, sometimes in large family groups. Those who could swim well would make their way out to the diving float and practice their swan dive, or jack knife, or perhaps perfect their belly flop. Tire inner tubes were popular individual floats that added to the joys of summer play.

These ladies and their children stand by the entrance sign to Willow Point Resort in Lakeport on the edge of Clear Lake.

These people are gathered at the Willow Point lakeshore to watch the activities on Clear Lake. Motorboat races were popular and attracted large crowds beginning in the 1930s, and on holiday weekends, there were boat parades and fireworks.

The above photograph shows the Benvenue Pavilion and Hotel about 1910. A *San Francisco Examiner* advertisement on July 28, 1910, read: "The Benvenue, Lakeport, Lake County, California. Hotel, Cottages, tents, private baths; cuisine and all service unsurpassed. First Class headquarters for Lake County tourists and auto parties. D. W. Dillard lessee and manager." The pavilion was built in 1898 by the Benvenue owners, Mr. and Mrs. Frank Scales, with a dance hall, a boat, and bathhouses. It was destroyed in 1910 by a storm, and in 1916, the hotel closed and was torn down. The pavilion sat across the street from St. Mary's Church in Lakeport.

The early roads were built by private land owners, and they collected toll at strategic stops from all who used their roads. The above photograph of Glen Alpine Springs shows the tollhouse that stood on the western bank of Scott Creek, six miles southwest of Lakeport, on the toll road coming from Hopland. Wagons and stages stopped to pay the toll and rest at the roadhouse owned by Ida Neal before continuing on to Lakeport, where they could change to a boat to cross the lake or to other stages traveling north or south. Glen Alpine had two developed springs with cemented basins and moderately carbonated water from which travelers could drink. By 1909, the property was deserted.

Pictured above is the Highland Springs tollhouse.

Four

EAST AND SOUTH LAKESHORES

CLEAR LAKE LODGE-LAKE CO. CAL

All around Clear Lake, resorts of varying sizes were drawing tourists into the county for the wonderful recreational pleasures afforded by the clear skies, balmy air, and inviting waters of the lake. With the coming of the automobile and improved roads, dozens of resorts were built in what were once the more remote areas, and the east- and south-shore businesses began to flourish. On the east side of the lake, in the area that was to become Nice, the Clear Lake Lodge was established from the Brown mansion. J. Dalzell Brown, who was president of the California Savings and Loan Association, began building his mansion in 1906; however, he embezzled funds, was convicted, and went to jail, leaving his mansion unfinished. From 1915 to 1917, it was used as a YMCA summer camp. Henry Springe became the owner, and for a time, the mansion was operated as the Lakeshore Villa. In 1921, much of the land around the mansion was sold for summer homes and grew into the town of Nice. During these years, the mansion was completed and became the Clear Lake Lodge. The above photograph shows the lodge about 1936. In 1996, it was purchased by World Mark and developed into timeshare units.

The above photograph, taken from a postcard mailed in 1947, shows Hendrick's Oak Haven in Lucerne. Oak Haven operated a group of tourist cabins along the edge of the lake.

The Bar B Marina in Nice sat along the shores of Clear Lake and accommodated tourists who brought their own boats for fishing and fun on the lake.

LUCERNE----
THE ALL-YEAR RESORT BEAUTIFUL

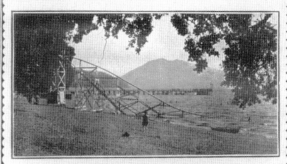

CALIFORNIA'S POPULAR PLAYGROUND, 100 miles north of Santa Francisco. Three hours from Sacramento via the new Tahoe-Ukiah highway; four hours from Oakland via Carquinez Bridge; via N. W. P. Ry. to Ukiah and Pickwick Stages to Lucerne; Pickwick Stages San Francisco to Lucerne.

Less Than One Hour by Air from Oakland, San Francisco or Sacramento to Lucerne's Splendid New Airport

All forms of outdoor recreation: Hunting, fishing, swimming, boating, golf, tennis, bridle paths, dancing, etc. Splendid new Hotel, ballroom, Bath House, modern cottages, U. S. post office, stores, cafes, etc.

RATES: Cottages, $1.50 to $2.50 per Day and up, per person.

Special Rates by Week and Month
Meals at Moderate Prices

For further information communicate with
MANAGER, LUCERNE COTTAGES
LUCERNE - LAKE COUNTY - CALIFORNIA

The advertisement on the right is from a 1930s Lake County Chamber of Commerce flier.

Laurel Beach, on the shores of Clear Lake's east side at the community of Nice, was a grand place for lake fishing, as these photographs attest. Catfish and bass were plentiful and delicious.

This is an early view of the cabins at Laurel Beach.

This view of Laurel Beach was taken about 1924.

The above photograph shows an overview of Austin's Beach at Lower Lake.

Austin's Clear Lake Resort

LOWER LAKE, CALIFORNIA

"A Safe Place to Send Your Family"

Boating - Bathing - Fishing - Hunting - Saddle
Horses - Tennis - Musical Entertainment
and Dancing Every Night

RUSTIC CAFE AND CABINS

with or without housekeeping equipment

This advertisement was in a Lake County Chamber of Commerce folder from 1930.

This 1925 view shows the huge trees that shaded Austin's Beach.

Highland's Court was one of the many small housekeeping resorts along the south shores of Clear Lake.

Jago's Resort was built by Louis Jago, who constructed cabins near his summer home to accommodate guests who came to Clear Lake to fish. He built a road in 1914 and over the next 20 years constructed 10 cottages and a general merchandise store. This store was originally in Lower Lake but was moved piece by piece to the resort site at the Jago Bay area. By 1946, his son John, with his wife Irene, took over the resort. Guests came to enjoy the beautiful area, fish, swim, and relax. In 1967, John and Irene Jago subdivided the resort property and sold all the cottages as summer homes. These pictures show the resort and John Jago in the rowboat in the picture below.

LOG TAVERN

CLEAR LAKE PARK, LAKE COUNTY, CALIFORNIA

Situated on the Shore of Clear Lake
"The Lake of Heart's Desire"

Within easy access over excellent roads from all points. Three and one-half hours drive from the Bay Region and Sacramento.

Diversions for every hour: Swimming, Fishing, Boating, Hunting, Horseback Riding, and Tennis.

You will find the rooms modern and comfortable and the meals excellent with a high standard of service. Here, also, you may rent cottages on the lake front by the day, week or month, with or without housekeeping equipment.

American and European plan

To Enjoy Beautiful Clear Lake at Its Best—Is to Stay at the

LOG TAVERN

P. O. Clearlake, California   **Phone Clear Lake Park**

The above advertisement for the Log Tavern is from a 1930 vacation guide published by Peck-Judah Travel Agency.

The above photograph is of the California Camera Club on an outing near Lower Lake in 1918.

Five

KELSEYVILLE REGION

In this area, the early resorts that developed were east or west of the town of Kelseyville. To the west sat Highland Springs, once one of the premier resorts for those looking for health cures. A hunter named Ripley claimed the area that was to become known as Highland Springs and built a cabin about 1860. He sold the property to H. H. Nunnally, who sold to Dr. A. B. Caldwell, who began building in 1871. Dr. Caldwell sold to Hiram Shartzer and S. M. Putnam in 1872, and they finished a large hotel and five cottages and could accommodate 60 guests by 1875. Shartzer bought out Putnam, but eight years later, Joseph Craig was owner and had enlarged the hotel, built an annex, and could accommodate several hundred people. The photograph above shows the stage at Highland Springs.

The Highland Springs resort sat in a lovely valley on 2,500 acres of wooded terrain with a flowing creek and numerous mineral springs. It offered many recreational facilities, such as the croquet court shown above and the pool shown below. It also had a bowling alley, tennis courts, stables for riding horses, dancing, hunting, fishing, and unending hiking trails.

Pictured are early guests at Highland Springs enjoying the beautiful grounds.

In the early years, the stage came about three times a week, bringing tourists and mail. However, the guests were never out of touch with their homes or businesses, as there were telegraph lines available for emergencies.

Highland Springs' many springs were the resort's most important features. In an early brochure, it listed the medicinal properties of seven of its main springs. Each was named and its curative powers for specific ailments listed. The Diana was used for treatment of blood, skin, and catarrhal troubles. The Neptune was good for chronic constipation, diarrhea, and as an anti-fat treatment. The Dutch was claimed to possess remarkable curative properties in diseases of the liver, kidneys, and nervous system. The Magic effected a cure for rheumatism. The Seltzer was famous for diseases requiring antacid, diuretic, and tonic treatment and was beneficial for dyspepsia, gout, neuralgia, sciatica, Bright's disease, diabetes, and catarrh of the bladder, gravel, and stone. One pint before meals was recommended for kidney and bladder derangement. The Kidney was used for inaction of the kidneys, and the Sulphur acted as a laxative. Guests were encouraged to drink and bathe in the water. These views show guests gathered at two of the springhouses.

The Seltzer spring was not only famous for its curative powers, but was also a favorite of guests and locals alike, who would squeeze lemons and add the juice to this natural sparkling water and considered it the "finest lemonade made." Gentlemen sit at the springhouse over the Seltzer spring to the right.

This overview of the Highland Springs resort gives an idea of the size of the establishment that grew up around the hotels. Thousands of summer visitors looking for health or recreational facilities visited the elegant old resort. After the 1920s, the resort began to fade, and it was eventually abandoned.

In the 1960s, Lake County took over the property and tore down all that was left of old Highland Springs resort. They built the Highland Springs Dam, and today what was once one of Lake County's grand resorts rests at the bottom of Highland Springs Lake in a recreational area owned by the county.

Soda Bay Resort, to the east of Kelseyville, was built by Capt. John Behr and operated by Captain Small beginning about 1872. In 1874, the property was sold to Mr. Souther who built a hotel with reading room, dining room, billiard room, and more cottages. He sold to Rev. Richard Wylie, who enlarged the hotel and added the bathhouse, bowling alley, ballroom, and more cottages. The photograph to the right shows guests with their fish catch on the steps of the hotel about 1918.

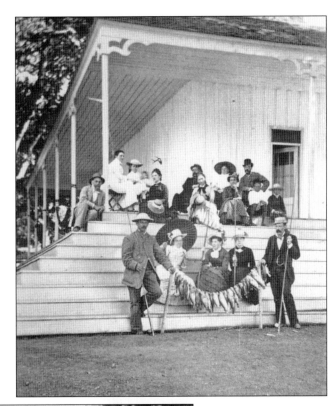

Pictured to the left are guests standing on the steps of the Soda Bay Resort hotel in 1918.

This bathhouse was built over a hot spring called Geyser Spring, Omar-Ach-Hah-Bee, or the Great Spring, producing several hundred gallons per minute of 87-degree water. It was located about 200 yards from the shore at Soda Bay among rocks that form a small island and was enjoyed by bathers who would go to the island by boat.

These guests at Soda Bay Resort gather on the pier, where they can take a boat out to the bathhouse over the large spring. There were a number of other smaller, warm bubbling springs for about a half-mile along the shore of the bay. Two formed carbonated drinking pools, but seasonal fluxion of Clear Lake would sometimes cover these springs, leaving only the iron stains showing on the rocky beach edges.

By 1928, Soda Bay Resort had been sold to developers, and the property was subdivided. By the 1950s, a number of small resorts interspersed with homes were built along the shores of the bay. The above photograph shows Betty Lou's Restaurant at Soda Bay in the 1950s.

This is an early photograph of the Soda Bay Resort hotel.

Above are the grounds at Edgewater Resort.

Edgewater Resort, shown in the 1950s, was among those resorts with housekeeping cabins that were built at Soda Bay.

The Red Barn Restaurant at Edgewater Resort was a landmark that prospered for many years at Soda Bay. This photograph is from the 1950s.

During the summer months, motorboat races were held at various locations on Clear Lake. This photograph shows the pier at Edgewater Resort at Soda Bay during a racing event in the 1950s.

These photographs show Carlsbad Springs in 1893, when it was operating as a small resort located four and a half miles south of Kelseyville near the Kelseyville-Middletown Road on Cole Creek. There were five springs within 100 yards of the hotel. The principle one was known as Arsenic Spring, with 74-degree carbonated water. Water was piped to a small bathhouse from a second spring yielding two gallons per minute, and two other springs were developed for drinking. In 1905, a brush fire destroyed the hotel building.

Six

COBB VALLEY

In the Cobb Valley area, one of the earliest resorts without any hot springs, had its beginnings as a stage stop halfway between Middletown and Lakeport at Glenbrook. Other small campgrounds and housekeeping facilities were developed over the years, but most are only a memory. Pine Grove is the one exception, as it is still a thriving business. This overview of Glenbrook Resort was taken around 1881. In 1869, William Bassett and Silas Broadwell bought the Glenbrook site in Cobb Valley and built a stage station, houses, and stock buildings; by 1871 there were accommodations for 100 guests, and Glenbrook had become a resort. William Bassett ran the operation for the next 25 years, claiming Glenbrook to be a health resort offering fine scenery, hunting, fishing, and an excellent table. The stage brought guests and the mail three times a week. The surrounding community of 200 included: Joe Bigwood, blacksmith; H. C. Boggs, lumber dealer and manufacturer; T. Caldwell, stock raiser; John Helbourn, lumber manufacturer; Joseph Hoffman, stock raiser; C. L. Howard, fruit grower; G. Kearn, fruit grower; Daniel King, dairy; B. Sherwood, lumber manufacturer; L. Yates, fruit grower; H. Young, meat market; John Moser, hotel; and William Bassett, postmaster and resort proprietor. Around 1900, the resort was operated by Orvis Treadway and by then George and Sadie Farley.

The above photograph shows an early view of Glenbrook Resort cabins. The stage stopped coming to Glenbrook in 1911 when the post office moved to Cobb and another road toward Lakeport opened, the but resort continued to operate for many years.

The entrance to Glenbrook Resort is pictured. Alfred J. Tantarelli and his wife, Opal R. Tantarelli, purchased the property in 1958 when it was no longer a resort.

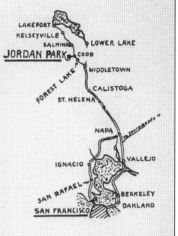
The advertisement above and the postcard with multiple views below are of Jordan Park in Cobb Valley, built around 1930. Dr. Ora Jordan and his wife, Elizabeth Presley, bought 485 acres in 1920 in Cobb Valley. Dr. Jordan lived in the Bay Area, but he hoped to build a golf course on the property. However, he was very allergic to poison oak, which was abundant on the property, so he cancelled his plans. Later his daughter, Sada, and her husband, Dr. Walter E. Smith, started the Jordan Park resort. They had a pool, cabins, and campgrounds and emphasized healthy living.

This photograph shows all that remains of the old Astorg Springs Hotel building, an example of one of the many small Lake County springs operations that sprang up before 1900 and disappeared within a decade or two. Astorg Springs was located three quarters of a mile southeast of Glenbrook Resort in Cobb Valley. The water was originally discovered when a tunnel was dug into the hillside as part of mining enterprise. Mining was abandoned, but the water was shipped in tanks to San Francisco, carbonated, and sold as table water for a period of time. It was called "chemise" water locally, as some thought it tasted like the chemise brush roots. The property today is owned by Mount Cobb SAC SHO Zen JE.

This photograph shows Pine Grove Camp's store as it looked in the 1920s. Morgan Noah Young and Margaret, his wife, are noted in the 1880 census of Cobb Valley with their seven children. Morgan Young died in 1886, and Margaret, then a widow with 10 children, started Young's Camp Ground, which would later become Pine Grove. In 1921, Margaret sold the property to Lynda Brow Egan and Julia Bishop Egan of Alameda County. The Egans made many improvements over the years, including a pool and cabins. Lynda Egan was the mother of Leslie Egan, and Julia Egan was the mother of Herbert Egan; the two women, together with their children, ran the business until they sold the property to Frank and Betty Frates in 1953. For 22 years, the Frateses operated the resort with the aid of their children, and in 1975, they retired and sold it to Robert and Roberta Grahn. Today the resort is owned and operated by Chris Layton. The resort catered to families and offered housekeeping cabins in a lovely wooded area with gurgling Kelsey Creek for fishing or exploring. They provided a ball diamond, horseshoes, ping-pong, and other entertainments. It became a community magnet for bingo players, tourists and locals alike, who would gather in the recreation room on warm evenings for camaraderie and fun.

This picture shows beautiful Kelsey Creek at the Pine Grove resort in Cobb Valley.

The pool at the Pine Grove resort is pictured above.

Seven

COBB AREA

The Cobb area contained a variety of resorts from the earliest years of resort development in Lake County. Seigler Springs, Howard Springs, Bonanza Springs, and Adams Springs were established in the 1870s, and Hobergs, probably the largest resort in Lake County without any mineral springs, began in the late 1890s. By the 1920s and 1930s, many smaller resorts were established in the mountains around Cobb, some with housekeeping facilities and campgrounds, some with pools, and all with access to the wonderful pine forests that cover the area. Above is the stage arriving at Seigler Springs, one of the earliest mineral-spring health establishments that added recreational and entertainment attractions and which was open to the public for over 100 years.

This picture shows tents set up on permanent platforms in the Seiglers camp grounds. The area was developed in the early years, before many cabins were built, and provided inexpensive sleeping quarters for guests who came to use the various spring waters.

The photograph above was taken prior to 1920 of Seiglers guests by the hotel. The simple wood supports of the hotel porch have been replaced by stone. The dining room was built completely of stone, and in later years, a large complex containing a recreation room, bar, coffee shop, and dance hall was constructed of stone. These buildings stayed quite cool during the summer heat.

This photograph taken c. 1920 shows Seiglers guests outside their cottage.

The lucky children pictured above got to go for a ride pulled by a dog team. The photograph is dated August 10, 1916, at Seigler Springs.

The early Seiglers owners raised many crops for the animals they kept and to supply guests with fresh food. Here they are haying in an area just below the main resort buildings.

These guests pose by their car in front of the Seigler Springs hotel. The child in the back seat is holding up her Kewpie doll, a very popular toy of that era.

Above is a carload of ladies in front of the Seigler Hotel.

This photograph shows guests on the path to the outdoor swimming pool posing by the big sulfur-iron-magnesia hot spring that was 138 degrees. Indigenous peoples in earlier times used this basin as a communal bath and called it *conotok*, meaning "white appearance of the ground."

The outdoor pool was fed by both hot and cold natural spring water. By controlling the amount of flow, the resort controlled the temperature of the water. The changing rooms are seen behind the pool above.

These gentlemen are gathered around one of the many springs at Seiglers. The resort property contained 660 acres, but most of the springs were within the 5-acre area that encompassed the resort proper. By 1909, thirteen springs were improved for use. Six were smaller flows from 68 degrees to 107 degrees and used for drinking.

These gentlemen are seated on the edge of the Magnesia Spring house. The water, at 64 degrees, was used for drinking, and it yielded up to two gallons per minute. Below are two ladies sitting in one of the springhouses. There was a Hot Geyser spring with 98-degree water that was developed by sinking a three-inch casing 90 feet deep; it was called Hot Geyser because it spouted once a day. However, after the 1906 earthquake, this action ceased. Another spring, known as the Arsenic Spring, yielded about five gallons per minute of 96-degree water and was used for drinking and bathing. Two additional springs with about the same flow but warmer water supplied the Hot Iron baths. The two hottest springs, with water over 119 and 126 degrees and with flows of 13 gallons per minute, issue from the edge of Seigler Creek and were used to supply tub baths.

Fishing was enjoyed by many guests, as attested by these photographs. There were two creeks running through the Seiglers property that held abundant fish, and the guests could also fish in Clear Lake by traveling five miles from the resort.

Game was abundant for those who enjoyed hunting. In the above photograph, guests gather to admire the hunter's luck. Below, the guests are enjoying a deer-meat barbecue under the oaks.

The California Camera Club band is posing with guests at a 1918 barbecue under the oaks at Seigler Springs.

In 1924, an orchestra assembled in the barbecue area at Seigler Springs to entertain the guests.

The California Camera Club called this group the Soup Marines. They are dressed in their bathing costumes lined up for the photographer near the Seiglers pool in 1918.

Relaxing in their home away from home, these guests pose by their cabin, called Meadow View.

Seiglers guests often enjoyed a day's trip to Clear Lake for a boat ride. The photograph above shows guests in 1920 on a pier at Clear Lake, and the photograph below shows 1940s guests enjoying the same type of outing. In the 1940s picture, the woman in white shorts standing third from the right in front is Dorothy Olsen, co-owner of Seigler Springs.

This picture shows Pioneer Charter buses at Seigler Springs in the 1930s.

The above photograph was taken in the 1930s of Seiglers guests sitting on the hotel steps. Two of the resort's owners are shown in the picture: Capt. Gudmund Olsen is seated in front on the far right, and Frank Hoberg is the man seated in the center reading a paper.

This photograph from the 1940s shows the dining room waitresses with Ernest Olsen standing in back center and Dorothy Olsen seated in front with two of their daughters, Claire on the left and Darlene far right.

This is the way the indoor pool looked in 1952. The water was naturally heated spring water, as warm as a pleasant bath.

The outdoor pool was a swimmer's delight. Filled with natural spring waters, it was clear and contained less bacteria than any other swimming pool of its day. The temperature was controlled by the amount of hot and cold spring water that flowed continually into the pool. This photograph is from the 1950s.

The Roman Baths at Seigler were in the same building as the indoor hot pool. A strolling accordion player is entertaining the sunbathers.

This view of the grounds at Seigler Springs shows some of the buildings with multiple rooms and the beautiful tree-lined walks edged with native stone that helped to make this resort such a pleasurable vacation destination.

The bar at Seiglers was underneath the recreation room and coffee shop and was built of native stone. It was always cool, even on the warmest days, and was a popular place for guests to gather for a cocktail before dinner.

These are 1950s views of the coffee shop and soda fountain. The room included a pool table for guests' pleasure, and they could check out tennis racquets and ping-pong equipment or put a nickel in the jukebox.

This lovely view of the Seigler Springs dining room shows guests enjoying dinner while being entertained by a strolling accordionist. The dining room seated 250 guests and was built of stone, keeping the room cool on hot summer days.

This 1950s picture shows the chef and his cooks, who were an important part of the vacation experience at Seiglers. They provided gourmet meals three times every day. The resort operated on the American plan, which meant the rates included meals.

The above cabin at Seigler Springs was named S.S. Acme in honor of Capt. Gudmund "Midnight" Olsen. Before Captain Olsen became an owner of Seigler Springs, he owned a lumber schooner called the SS *Acme*, which sailed the Pacific coastal waters. He came from Norway as a young man of 15 in 1892 and worked as a seaman along the California coast. Eventually he was able to own his own boat, and he earned the title Midnight during his career because of his ability to go in and out of treacherous harbor waters, such as those at Eureka, even at midnight, and not have to wait until dawn as other boat captains usually did. He was well known up and down the Pacific Coast for his expertise, and his name is recorded in many shipping records of that era. He retired around 1930, and he and his wife were partners with their son and daughter-in-law, Ernest and Dorothy Olsen, at Seigler Springs until his death in 1958.

A full-time masseuse was available to the Seiglers guests during the summer months. Dr. Bojorques and his nurse pose on the porch of the massage parlor shown above.

The Catholic church supplied a priest for summer services at this charming chapel at Seigler Springs. This 1950s photograph shows guests leaving the chapel on a lovely summer Sunday morning.

Howard Springs called itself "Nature's Mysterious Laboratory," and claimed a quick and permanent cure for 17 different diseases as well as all diseases of the stomach, liver, kidneys, and blood. The springs were discovered in 1877 by C. W. Howard, who patented 160 acres of property containing 42 hot and cold springs. They are located two miles southeast from Seigler Springs and five miles north of Harbin Springs, about six miles from Lower Lake. A hotel, cabins, and campsites were built, and the most important springs were developed for drinking and bathing, with temperatures ranging from 50 to 110 degrees. The largest of the hot springs were piped into tubs, and a hot soda-sulfur spring supplied a plunge bath. Water from springs called Lithia, Bohemia, and Eureka were bottled and sold for table use for a period of time prior to 1905. Two springs called "twins" were six feet apart, and one was 50 degrees, the other 102 degrees. They claimed the world's largest combination of natural mineral waters. The resort passed through many owners and was closed to the public by 1969, when the Pappas family owned the property. Pictured above is the hotel, and to the right is an overview of the early resort.

The above photograph shows the pool at Howard Springs about 1950.

This view of Howard Springs shows guests by the Iron-Sulphur and Borax bathhouses in the 1950s.

Bonanza Springs was operated as a mineral springs resort by Henry Fern as early as 1882. There are three springs known as Sulphur, Soda, and Iron situated in a grove on a gentle slope bordering a ravine about three miles northeast of Adams Springs and halfway between Seiglers and Howard Springs. By 1910, the property was owned by C. N. E. Enret and H. Penning, and the large hotel had been destroyed by fire, leaving only 8 or 10 cottages and the tent grounds. The Sulphur spring was a covered well 9 feet deep from which water was piped to a latticed house. The Soda and Iron springs issued from crevices below the Sulphur House. All three were cold and small, yielding about a half-gallon per minute. A new hotel was built in the mid-1920s, and Fred Laier built several stone buildings. The resort prospered until the hotel burned in the 1930s. Bonanza Springs never recovered. The property changed hands from time to time, and in the 1960s, a religious cult called Hindu Mystics headed by Father Subrayana purchased the property and held art and music classes. The photograph above is of the early Bonanza Springs campgrounds.

Loch Lomond Resort was built at the junction of Highway 175 and Seigler Canyon Road, three miles north of Cobb Village, and was named for a very small wet-weather lake to the north of the main building. There were housekeeping cabins and a campground, and the main building included a very popular dining room and bar, a grocery store, and a gas station. In the late 1950s, a modern swimming pool was built across the highway that ran through the resort. A fire destroyed the main building, and the owners rebuilt by the swimming pool. The area around the resort has been subdivided, and there are many summer and permanent homes. The owners still operate a grocery store, bar, and restaurant. These pictures show the resort from the early 1950s.

This photograph shows the Loch Lomond store, restaurant, and bar as it looks today.

Salimina's Resort, pictured above, was built by the Salimina family on their ranch north of Cobb Mountain on the main highway to Kelseyville. They offered housekeeping cabins, horseback riding, swimming, and a restaurant and bar in a charming wooded setting.

NESTLING among the giant pines, firs and oaks, high in the mountains of scenic Lake County, is SALMINA'S RESORT, one of the most popular and best-known vacation spots in this favored part of the state.

At an elevation of 2800 feet, the mountain breezes are cool and invigorating. The days are warm, but never sultry, and the nights are cool.

The scenery is an everlasting delight to vacationers, the climate is ideal for pleasure-seekers, and the Resort is a wonderful place to relax and enjoy yourself.

Every effort is made to assure the comfort of guests; to offer entertainment and happy days in the mountains.

Clean rooms and comfortable beds bring rest to the tired pleasure-seekers.

We have been known for three generations for our fine Italian food.

Swimming — Bocce - Ball
Cocktail Lounge
and Many Other Amusements

Phone Cobb Exchange, 928-5230

Or Write Salmina's Resort

RESORT RATES

*

Salmina's Resort

LAKE COUNTY, CALIFORNIA

Located 100 Miles from the San Francisco Bay Area, 14 Miles North of Middletown on Highway 175; Turn left in Middletown at Standard Oil Service Station

Write

ESTER AND MARIO CIARDELLA
SALMINA'S RESORT

Route 1, Kelseyville, California
Or Phone Cobb Exchange,
928-5230

The brochure pictured above is for Salimina's Resort.

This overview of Adams Springs taken in 1910 shows the hotel and the annex, cabins, and many guests lined up for their photograph. These springs were discovered by Charles Adams in 1869 in a canyon of pines 11 miles north of Middletown and 2.5 miles from Seigler Springs. The four springs are all cool and carbonated. In 1871, Adams sold to the Whitten brothers, who built a main hotel, six cottages, and campgrounds. By 1888, the resort was owned by Dr. William R. Prather, and by the time the above photograph was taken, the resort could accommodate 400 people.

The stage has arrived at Adams Springs. Three times each week, horse-drawn conveyances arrived from Calistoga bringing guests and mail. Many of the guests came from the Bay Area, where they could take the ferry, then the train to Calistoga to meet the stage for Lake County. They traveled all day, and the trip over Mount Saint Helena on the stage road was dusty and rough, but they came by the thousands to enjoy all the resorts had to offer. Many would stay for a month or more.

This photograph from 1915 shows guests standing in the swimming pool at Adams Springs. The folks on the porch are in front of the pool dressing rooms.

This panoramic view of the Adams pool shows guest cottages on the right. The water in the pool was piped from one of the cool springs and was about 50 degrees during the summer.

Guests at Adams Springs walk in the hills close by.

Spur's Bull Moose Stage is parked in front of the Adams Springs hotel in this 1911 photograph.

This photograph shows the dining room at Adams Springs. They advertised a marvelous table.

The above photograph is of the hotel built in 1929 at Adams Springs. An article in the *Lake County Bee* in December of that year said: "The new hotel has a 900 foot porch, twelve feet wide, built around the entire structure, with 28 guest rooms." At that time, it was the most modern hotel in Lake County, with a large lobby, bar, coffee shop, and dining room.

On July 16, 1943, fire destroyed the new hotel at Adams Springs. It burned quickly because it was all-wood construction. The only casualty was a woman who went back to a second-story room to save her jewelry.

Adams Springs bottled and sold water throughout California and beyond. Their motto, "The Springs that made Lake County Famous," was based on the claims made of cures of stomach, liver, and kidney diseases by drinking Adams water. This advertisement is from a 1915 brochure.

Shown above are Carl Rudolph Gustav Hoberg and Emma Mathilde Stolzenwald in 1868. They moved to Lake County in 1885 with their five children and settled on the property in the Cobb area that was to become Hoberg's Resort. Gustav Hoberg immigrated to Chicago from Prussia in 1861, when he was 16. He served in the Union army the last months of the Civil War and an additional three years as a pony soldier touring the West. He and Mathilde lived for 15 years in New Holstein, Wisconsin, where he taught school and was a partner in a hardware store. In 1885, he and his brother-in-law, George Kammerer, who lived in San Francisco, obtained 300 acres of land near Cobb Mountain. Gustav planned to live on the land and improve it, and George was a silent partner. Gustav and Mathilde built their home, planted orchards and gardens, and were accommodating summer guests who camped and shared their table when Gustav died suddenly at age 50 in 1895. The oldest son, Max, continued to develop the resort with his mother. They built cabins and recreational facilities and by 1920 had built the hotel. Max married Thresa Bleuss in 1905, and they had four children. Sons George, Paul, and Frank grew up in the business and together with their wives would take over the responsibilities of the resort in the 1930s.

In the early years, the Hoberg family could accommodate only a small number of guests. Guests brought their own camping equipment and would eat in the family dining room or perhaps at tables under the pines. This photograph dated 1899 shows Mathilde Hoberg seated at the left rear, with her sister, Helene Kammerer, seated next to her. George Kammerer is seated at the far right. Note that on the ladies' table are coffee cups and cakes, and on the gentlemen's table are a bottle of liquor and glasses with a bucket by their feet with more drinks.

Hiking to Sunset Rock was a planned activity by nearly all of the guests who visited Hoberg's Resort, and often a group photograph would be taken. The young man sitting at the top right is Arthur Hoberg.

Max Hoberg is sitting on the hood of a guest's car at Hoberg's Resort.

These guests are gathered on the steps of the resort dining room for a group photograph to remember their vacation at Hoberg's. This picture was taken about 1915, when meals would have been 50¢ per day for three meals, served family style. The dining room held 60 guests, and almost all of the food was from the family gardens and livestock.

The first swimming pool, shown above, was down a path through the pines about a quarter of a mile from the resort. The water came from a spring and was pure and cold. In an early brochure, Hoberg's advertised that mosquitoes and poison oak were rare.

Shown above is the Hoberg's hotel lobby in the 1920s. The photograph over the piano shows Luther Burbank at Sun Rise Rock, a short hike from the resort. To the right of the piano is a music box with tin records that could be played.

Luther Burbank, the renowned "plant wizard" of Santa Rosa, stayed at Hoberg's Resort a number of times in the early 1920s. He is seated at the croquet court in front of the hotel. He and his wife and niece always stayed in the Spring cabin.

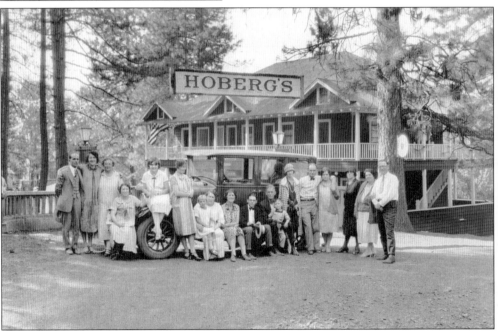

These guests pose in front of the hotel with Theresa Hoberg, seated in the center with daughter Matilda on her lap, about 1920.

The guests in this 1920s photograph have dressed like ladies in a harem by using dining-room napkins for veils. Hoberg's Resort continued to grow over the years, as they added over 90 cabins and a dozen buildings with multiple units. There was a grand tiled swimming pool, grass park and game field, large dance hall under the stars, two bars, barbershop, beauty shop, coffee shop, and a dining room, and the hotel included a small dance floor with piano bar, meeting rooms, and recreation rooms. People flocked to Hoberg's to join the fun, and the activities almost never stopped. During World War II, they came to enjoy the sunshine and to escape the 24-hour schedules driving the Bay Area's shipyards and war production efforts.

This late-1940s photograph shows guests enjoying a cocktail party in the Pine Bowl, the outdoor dance pavilion, during a convention at Hoberg's.

This photograph of the staff on the steps of the dining room was taken in 1936 and shows waitresses and busboys with Annette Hoberg (far right not in uniform), who was hostess of the dining room from 1932 to 1956. Many of these employees were local teenagers who came to work the summers and spring and fall weekends.

The interior of Hoberg's coffee shop was built of beautiful knotty pine, a very popular decorative wood of that time. The resort was operated on the American plan, which meant that meals were included in the rates; however, the coffee shop served those who wanted extra food or fountain service throughout the day, and it was kept very busy during and after the dance hours in the evenings. To the far left, the Upper Bar can be seen. The Lower Bar was underneath the lobby of the hotel.

These two photographs were taken at the dedication of the Paul Hoberg Airport in 1947. The runway was 5,000 feet long, 125 feet wide, fully paved, and capable of landing commercial airplanes. A DC-3 Western Airlines cargo carrier flew out with a cargo of Lake County Bartlett pears at the dedication flight. In attendance were 2,250 people plus 102 airplanes. Both Frank and George Hoberg owned small four passenger planes and flew guests to and from Lake County. The airport is located five miles southeast of Hoberg's Resort just below Seigler Springs Resort.

In this picture taken at the Paul Hoberg Airport dedication in 1947, the pilots, cabin crew, and Seigler Springs dining room waitresses pose with George Hoberg (far left), Jane Hoberg (daughter of Paul Hoberg, third from the right), and Dorothy Olsen (second from the right).

Peck-Judah Travel Agency made travel arrangements for tourists who wished to travel to Lake County as early as 1900. This photograph shows their window display in Los Angeles during the 1950s.

The Freddie Martin Band, shown above, played at Hoberg's Pine Bowl dance floor in 1947. Martin, known as "Mr. Silvertone" for his pleasant, relaxed, sweet-tone music, played tenor sax. The man seated on the right is Merv Griffin, who toured for four years as a singer with the Freddie Martin Band.

In 1946, the Redwood Empire Association met at Hoberg's for its annual meeting and weekend of dinners, parties, recreation, and business. Their program included the noted gentlemen above. From left to right are Roger Lapham, mayor of San Francisco; George Hoberg, resort owner and Redwood Empire Association president; Earl Warren, governor of California; H. H. Arnold, general in the U.S. Army; and Leo Carrillo, Hollywood actor.

Ex-heavyweight champion Max Baer, seated in the center in Western dress, visited Hoberg's Resort in 1940 and caused quite a stir. Known as the Livermore Larruper, he was reported to have the most powerful right hand in history. He knocked out 50 men during his boxing career and was heavyweight champion of the world for 364 days by knocking out Primo Camera on June 14, 1934. He lost the title to Jimmy Braddock on June 13, 1935. While he was at Hoberg's, he chatted with guests throughout the evening and posed for photographs. In this photograph, George Hoberg is seated second from the left.

The family always ate their meals in the dining room with the guests. This photograph from the early 1940s shows Max and Theresa Hoberg enjoying dinner surrounded by guests. After Max and Theresa turned the management of the resort over to their sons and their wives, they were still very visible and involved around the resort.

Contest winners from the 1950s television program *Queen for a Day* are shown with George Hoberg on their arrival at the resort. To become "Queen for a Day," contestants would relate why they were worthy of winning, usually a hard-luck tale, and the audience would pick a winner. Along with other prizes, they could win an all-expense-paid vacation at Hoberg's Resort.

Gov. Earl Warren is shaking hands with a guest on the steps of the resort dining room while Frank Hoberg looks on.

These young women are seated at the edge of Hoberg's pool, built in the late 1930s. Master of ceremonies Ozzie Coulthart (with his trumpet) organized swimming contests for the children every afternoon. The pool was surrounded by acres of lawn where guests played softball and sunbathed. To the north of the pool was the tennis court, and nearby was a playground for the kiddies. In the 1950s, a children's pool was added.

On amateur show night, everyone got into the act. This group of dining room waitresses in their uniforms are dancing and singing to the tune of "Dinah," with lyrics rewritten about Hoberg's. From left to right are Ozzie Coulthart, Betty Long, Myrtle Zupont, Mary Fraiser, Polly Stansil, unidentified, Sonny Becco, Barbara Junkin, and an unidentified man.

In 1950, Xavier Cugat brought his orchestra and entourage to Hoberg's, drawing a huge crowd to the Pine Bowl for dancing and revelry. Here Cugat and Abbe Lane, who was a singer with the band and one of Cugat's five wives, pose for a fun photograph with one of Gustav Hoberg's great-grandsons, Don Hoberg.

Tennessee Ernie Ford came to play golf at the Hoberg's Forest Lake Golf Course in 1956. He is shown on the left with Bill Angelley. Ford is probably best remembered for his recording of "Sixteen Tons," which was released that same year as a single and sold one million copies in 24 days, setting a record to that date.

Tommy Dorsey played at Hoberg's Pine Bowl in 1946. It was standing room only when Dorsey, Xavier Cugat, Freddy Martin, Harry James, and others came to entertain on summer weekends. The dance floor was open to the stars and the music could be heard for some distance, so people danced all over the resort grounds to that magical swing when the floors were jammed.

When visiting bands came to Hoberg's for the weekend, the band members often took advantage of the facilities such as swimming and games with the guests. In this photograph, Tommy Dorsey has joined the guest softball team and is trying his hand with the bat. Sal Carson is catcher for the Hoberg team, and Frank Hoberg is umpire. Sometimes a team would come from Seigler Springs made up of staff and guests to challenge the Hoberg team. A lot of good-natured rivalry developed, and some guests came year after year prepared to play and hoping to be on the winning team.

Sal Carson and his orchestra played at Hoberg's for many seasons beginning in 1945. Sal, from the Bay Area, was known for his beautiful music. Those who danced to Sal's music remember a signature piece that he began most of his evenings with called "Honey Dear." He brought his orchestra to the resort around June 1 each summer, and they would play nightly under the stars at the Pine Bowl until Labor Day. The above photograph shows Sal with the band in front of the moon mural painted by Lee Fidge.

Wednesday was costume night, and many guests joined in the fun. Judging by applause would take place for the best or most inventive costume. The prize was always a bottle of champagne. If someone had a particularly bad costume, or if the crowd thought someone was misbehaving, that person would be carried over to the swimming pool and thrown in. It was all in good fun, and no one was ever injured by the pranksters, who made sure the victim could swim. This photograph was taken in 1948.

An evening ride into the forest and time for a bonfire and marshmallow roast made vacation memories for many Hoberg's guests. From left to right are Robert Richard, Barbara Smart, John Myers, Marilyn Hoberg, Don Hoberg, George Lee, Ann Hoberg, and two unidentified revelers in 1950.

Walt Tolleson and his band played at Hoberg's in the late 1950s. Master of ceremonies Ozzie Coulthart leads the band while Walt plays his trumpet. Tolleson was a popular bandleader in the San Francisco area for 45 years and played at various times at the resort. The busy years continued up to the 1960s, but gradually things changed at Hoberg's and the other large resorts in Lake County. Tourists were traveling farther and demanding more. Competitive convention facilities were being built in large cities throughout the state. The Hobergs began to face unconquerable financial difficulties. Paul Hoberg died in 1946, Frank Hoberg died in 1961, and George Hoberg died in 1970. For two years after George died, the family operated the facility as a boarding school, and in 1974, they sold to Maharishi International University.

Pictured above is Forest Lake Resort as it was in the 1950s. James Hartford Smith bought the property in 1868 and built his home where the main building stands now. When he died his son, Nate, lived in the house with his wife and ran a campground and rented to boarders. After 1900, the property passed to Nate's son, Will Smith, who sold to Hugh Davey, and he sold to Jim McCauley, who started a resort he named Camp Calso. He built cabins and around 1930 built the main building. In 1935, he put a dam in Kelsey Creek and created a lake. Pictured below is Camp Calso showing Kelsey Creek.

Shown is James B. McCauley, developer of Forest Lake Resort, at the dedication celebration of Lake McCauley in 1935. McCauley continued adding cabins, and he built a swimming pool in 1937. In 1938, the name Camp Calso was changed to Forest Lake Resort. Vince Emerson and his wife, Marian, ran the resort from 1939 until his death in 1946, after which the resort was managed by Marian and their son, Don Emerson. From 1950 to 1963, Don Emerson and his wife, Dorothy, owned and ran Forest Lake. They sold to Joe Breen and Vic Tamera. Today the property is owned by Calistoga Mineral Water, part of the Nestles Corporation.

This photograph, taken in 1954, shows the new Hoberg's Forest Lake Golf Course. The players are Dorothy Emerson on the left, Vernon Genesee, golf pro Gordon Ferris, and Bonnie ?, right.

Shown in the 1960s from left to right are Don Emerson, golf pro Gordon Ferris, George Hoberg, and Eddie Erdelatz, coach of the U.S. Navy football team at Annapolis and first coach of the Oakland Raiders.

Pictured above is the lovely Forest Lake Resort swimming pool in 1959. The child in front is Karen Emerson Ogando.

Posing for the camera in a mock baseball game are Y. A. Tittle of the 49ers at bat, Eddie Erdelatz catching, and Don Emerson acting as umpire. This photograph was taken at the Hoberg's Forest Lake golf course in 1960.

These vacationers are enjoying beautiful Forest Lake on a lovely summer day.

Guests from Forest Lake Resort are enjoying horseback riding along the shores of Forest Lake about 1959.

Forest Lake Resort provided many activities and facilities for families. Childcare was provided daily with supervised activities that included fun at the pool, games, and special meal times. This photograph shows children anticipating an evening hay ride.

Whispering Pines Resort was begun in the 1930s by the Strickler family and is successfully operating today, 77 years later. David and Lena Strickler and their children came to Lake County from Pennsylvania in 1896, and in 1902, they obtained 320 acres in the Cobb Mountain area. They made their living in the early years selling vegetables and wood at the nearby mercury mines. In 1927, with their son, Carl, and his wife, Grace, they opened the first general store in the area, and in 1935, a post office was established at the store, operating until 1962. The store building also housed a bar and coffee shop. The first log cabin for guests was built in the 1930s. They milled their own lumber and did all the construction themselves. The pool was dug by hand and was fed by natural spring water. Eventually this pool on the edge of the highway was filled in and a new pool constructed in the center of the resort. They continued building cabins and today have 29 housekeeping units. This family-owned resort has seen four generations of Stricklers: David and Lena, Carl and Grace, Donald and Madeline, and Steven and Michaela and their two sons, Jake and Zach. Above is the original store building with (from left to right) David and Lena Strickler, Neal ?, Katie ?, and Carl and Grace Strickler on the right on the porch.

This photograph shows Carl Strickler building one of the log cabins at Whispering Pines Resort.

Pictured above is a cabin at Whispering Pines Resort in the snow in the 1950s.

Whispering Pines Resort is closed for the winter.

Above is a photograph of the new store building at Whispering Pines.

This picture shows the first pool built at Whispering Pines Resort.

Pictured at Whispering Pines Resort in the 1960s are three generations of Stricklers after a successful deer hunt. Carl is on the left, Steve in the center, and Don on the right.

This photograph shows Cobb Mountain Lodge, one of the many small resorts that once were successful businesses in Lake County. Cobb Mountain Lodge was eight miles north of Middletown in the Cobb area, just south of Whispering Pines Resort. It was destroyed by fire in the early 1970s.

Eight

MIDDLETOWN REGION

Mineral springs resorts were established north of the town of Middletown along the Big Canyon Road area and to the northwest of the town just off the main highway going north to Lakeport, where Anderson Creek flows. These photographs of Harbin Springs, located six miles north of Middletown in Big Canyon, are from the early resort era. The property was claimed by Capt. A. A. Ritchie before Madison James Harbin purchased it sometime after 1856. Harbin operated a resort until 1868 then sold to R. Williams and J. Hughes, who enlarged the facilities to more than 25 buildings including a bathhouse containing nine tub baths, five plunges, and one mud bath. The spring waters were from 90 to 120 degrees and contained arsenic, iron, and sulfur, yielding up to 8.5 gallons per minute. In addition to accommodations for 200 people, there were a bar, dining room, steam room, barbershop, gym, and dance floor. In 1894, most of the buildings were destroyed by fire, but Williams began rebuilding, and with the aid of his son-in-law, who became manager, the resort was modernized and enlarged, eventually catering to families. The resort has passed through many owners and has been used at various times as a health or spiritual retreat center. Today it is operated by a New Age community. Above is a view of one of the Harbin Springs hotels.

This photograph shows the Harbin Springs swimming tank.

Above is Harbin Springs bathhouse in 1909.

E SHIP" ICE CREAM PARLOR AT STUPARICH RESORT, LAKE COUNTY, CAL.

The ice-cream parlor above was part of the Stuparich Resort, one mile from Harbin Springs. Paul and Stephen Stuparich purchased property adjoining Harbin Springs and began building a summer home in 1913. Paul lived in San Francisco with his family and was a building contractor. His brother Stephen lived in Middletown. After building a private residence, they began working on a hotel and guest buildings. The Stuparich Resort opened to the public in 1922 and was very modern and more elegant than Harbin. They prided themselves on their modern plumbing, which included Turkish baths, a hot plunge, a steam room, massage rooms, and ice water piped to every table in the dining room. They hired a European-trained chef who cooked gourmet meals. Their hotel and "bungalettes" could accommodate 85 people, and they had a dancing pavilion, game room, and swimming pool. In June 1926, after only three seasons, they were in financial trouble, and sold the resort and all their land to Victor Klinker, a senior vice president of Fleishhacker Interests. Klinker sold to Joseph Greenbach of San Francisco, who planned to continue running the resort, but in October 1928, a good part of Stuparich Resort burned to the ground. Greenbach sold to Newt Booth of Harbin in 1930, and the once wonderfully elaborate resort became part of Harbin Springs.

Anderson Springs is located at the head of Laconoma Valley, four miles north of Middletown. In 1873, Dr. Alex Anderson and Laban Patriquin, who lived with their families in Napa, came to the area while on a hunting trip. They found the eight springs and surrounding area so pleasant that they decided it would be a perfect place to build a health resort. They were able to obtain the property and over the next year built a hotel and developed the springs for drinking and bathing. In 1894, they opened the resort with hotel accommodations for 30 guests, hot and cold baths, and a campground. By the end of the first season, they had run out of money, and Laban Patriquin went to work at the Oat Hill quicksilver mine, where he became superintendent and worked for 10 years. Laban was married to Alexandre Anderson, daughter of Dr. Alex Anderson.

The old Anderson Springs hotel pictured was run by three of Dr. Anderson's daughters, Barbara, Joey, and Rose, for many years.

In this photograph of the Anderson family in their new car, old Dr. Anderson, with white moustache, is seated in the back seat, Walter Anderson, in a white shirt, is seated on the running board, and the woman farthest left is Dr. Charlotte Anderson.

Hiking around the springs was a favorite pastime. In this photograph is a group of guests resting at the falls above the resort.

Over the years, housekeeping cabins were added to the resort at Anderson Springs as well as recreational facilities such as croquet, horseshoes, skittles, and bowling.

This bridge over the creek is called Patriquin Bridge after one of the original owners, Laban Patriquin.

These three women enjoying a walk by the creek are, from left to right, Anna Aden, Lena Aden, and Dr. Belknap.

The boy in this photograph is Leonard Noble of the Noble family in Middletown, hunting in the Anderson Springs area.

The resort property was sold to A. R. Meade by the Anderson heirs, and he subdivided and sold to individual property owners. Above is an early photograph of the croquet court.

The old resort was popular for many years and some of the homes there now are owned by fourth-generation permanent and summer residents. There are over 50 year-round homes in the area, and the creek has been dammed to make a beautiful park-like pool area for the homeowners. The above wagon that once brought guests to Anderson Springs is long forgotten, as today's summer vacationers travel to Lake County in modern gas buggies whose only resemblance is their four wheels.

Pictured is a map of Lake County.

ACROSS AMERICA, PEOPLE ARE DISCOVERING SOMETHING WONDERFUL. THEIR HERITAGE.

Arcadia Publishing is the leading local history publisher in the United States. With more than 3,000 titles in print and hundreds of new titles released every year, Arcadia has extensive specialized experience chronicling the history of communities and celebrating America's hidden stories, bringing to life the people, places, and events from the past. To discover the history of other communities across the nation, please visit:

www.arcadiapublishing.com

Customized search tools allow you to find regional history books about the town where you grew up, the cities where your friends and family live, the town where your parents met, or even that retirement spot you've been dreaming about.

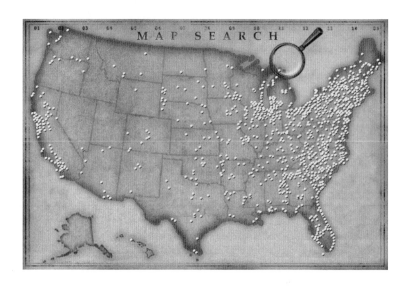